RANMA 1/2

VOL. 13
Action Edition

Story and Art by
RUMIKO TAKAHASHI

English Adaptation/Gerard Jones and Toshifumi Yoshida
Touch-Up Art & Lettering/Wayne Truman
Cover and Interior Design & Graphics/Yuki Ameda
Editor (1st Edition)/Trish Ledoux
Editor (Action Edition)/Avery Gotoh
Supervising Editor (Action Edition/Michelle Pangilinan

Managing Editor/Annette Roman
Director of Production/Noboru Watanabe
Editorial Director/Alvin Lu
Sr. Dir. of Licensing & Acquisitions/Rika Inouye
VP of Sales & Marketing/Liza Coppola
Executive Vice President/Hyoe Narita
Publisher/Seiji Horibuchi

For the purposes of publication in English, the artwork in this publication is printed in reverse from the original Japanese version.

Printed in Canada.

Published by VIZ, LLC
P.O. Box 77010
San Francisco, CA 94107

1st Edition Published 1999

Action Edition
10 9 8 7 6 5 4 3 2 1
First Printing, October 2004

Ranma 1/2™

VOL. 13 **Action Edition**

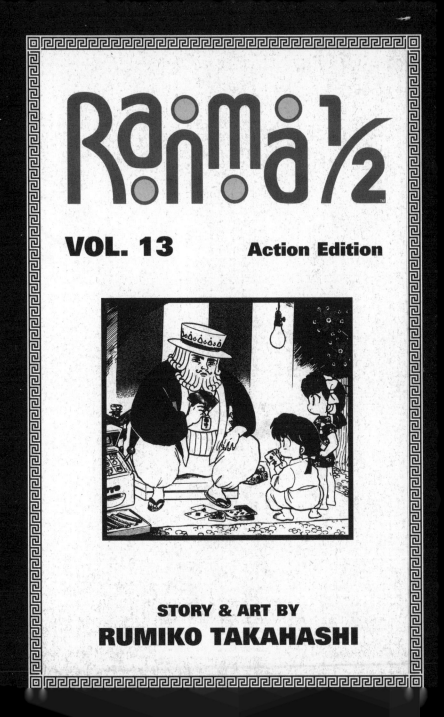

STORY & ART BY

RUMIKO TAKAHASHI

STORY THUS FAR

The Tendos are an average, run-of-the-mill Japanese family—on the surface, that is. Soun Tendo is the owner and proprietor of the Tendo Dojo, where "Anything-Goes Martial Arts" is practiced. Like the name says, anything goes, and usually does.

When Soun's old friend Genma Saotome comes to visit, Soun's three lovely young daughters—Akane, Nabiki, and Kasumi—are told that it's time for one of them to become the fiancée of Genma's teenaged son, as per an agreement made between the two fathers years ago. Youngest daughter Akane—who says she hates boys—is quickly nominated for bridal duty by her sisters.

Unfortunately, Ranma and his father have suffered a strange accident. While training in China, both plunged into one of many "cursed" springs at the legendary martial arts training ground of Jusenkyo. These springs transform the unlucky dunkee into whoever—or whatever—drowned there hundreds of years ago.

From then on, a splash of cold water turns Ranma's father into a giant panda, and Ranma becomes a beautiful, busty young woman. Hot water reverses the effect...but only until next time. As it turns out, Ranma and Genma aren't the only ones who have taken the Jusenkyo plunge—and it isn't long before they meet several other members of the Jusenkyo "cursed."

Although their parents are still determined to see Ranma and Akane marry and carry on the training hall, Ranma seems to have a strange talent for accumulating surplus fiancées...and Akane has a few stubbornly determined suitors of her own. Will the two ever work out their differences, get rid of all these "extra" people, or will they just call the whole thing off? What's a half-boy, half-girl (not to mention all-girl, *angry* girl) to do...?

CONTENTS

CAST OF CHARACTERS

RYOGA HIBIKI
Melancholy martial artist with no sense of direction, a hopeless crush on Akane, and a stubborn grudge against Ranma. Changes into a small, black pig Akane's named "P-chan."

RANMA SAOTOME
Martial artist with far too many fiancées and an ego that won't let him take defeat. Changes into a girl when splashed with cold water.

SHAMPOO
Chinese-Amazon warrior who's gone from wanting to kill Ranma to wanting to marry him. Changes into a cute kitty cat when splashed with water.

GENMA SAOTOME
Ranma's lazy father, who left his wife and home years ago with his young son (Ranma) to train in the martial arts. Changes into a panda.

COLOGNE
Shampoo's great-grandmother, a martial artist and matchmaker.

AKANE TENDO
Martial artist, tomboy, and Ranma's reluctant fiancée. Has no clue how much Ryoga likes her, or what relation he might have to her pet black pig, P-chan.

HAPPOSAI
Martial arts master who trained both Genma and Soun. Also a world-class pervert.

SOUN TENDO
Head of the Tendo household and owner of the Tendo Dojo.

TATEWAKI KUNO
Blustering upperclassman with a love of the ancient Japanese arts, Akane Tendo, and the mysterious "pig-tailed girl," who he has no idea is really girl-type Ranma.

UKYO KUONJI
Ranma's childhood friend. Has a flair for cooking and a dislike of Akane. Wields a mean spatula.

PART 1

THE MARK OF THE GODS

WHERE AM I NOW...?
SWIP
RRRSHLLL
HM ?
FOOOD!
ZHA
SHK

BWAK
DONK
GONK
FEH,
TRYING TO ATTACK ME...?
WHAT A FOOL-HARDY GUY.
FUMP
SQOOSH
HUH?
GWI
IT'S JUST A WITHERED OLD MAN...
FOOD..
BWACH BWACH
KIMEN SCHOOL OF MARTIAL ARTS CAL-LIGRAPHY?
RAMEN
CUP O' SQUID
CUP NOODLE
I AM A WELL KNOWN AND RESPECTED MARTIAL ARTS CALLIGRAPHER.
...NONE OTHER.
SHLUP SHLOP
SSSHHHHLLLORRPP
SUPER NOODLE
AND WHAT EXACTLY *IS* MARTIAL ARTS CAL-LIGRAPHY?

WHEW...
CHK CHK
POM POM
NOW THEN...
FFFWIP
WHAT ARE YOU DOING?
MOOSH...
IN RETURN FOR YOUR FOOD, I WAS GOING TO BESTOW UPON YOU MY MARTIAL ARTS CALLIGRAPHY.
A PERSON'S POWER COMES FROM THE HYPO-GASTRIC REGION...
...BASICALLY, THE ABDOMEN.
Hypogastrium Region
ESPECIALLY IN MARTIAL ARTS, IT'S IMPORTANT TO CONCENTRATE YOUR *CHI* IN YOUR ABDOMEN.
MARTIAL ARTS CALLIGRAPHY IS A TECHNIQUE WHICH, WHEN USED TO MARK A PERSON'S ABDOMEN WITH A SPECIAL SYMBOL...
SHWAAA...
...THAT PERSON CAN DRAW UPON INCREDIBLE STRENGTH...
SO IT'S A KIND OF CHARM?
GRRIK GRRIK
STICK O' INK

WHERE ARE YOU GOING?
FEH, HOW LAME...
SHF
DON'T YOU WANT TO BE THE STRONGEST MAN IN THE WORLD!?
TWITCH
STRONGEST IN THE WORLD...?
NOW EXPOSE YOUR ABDOMEN!
YOU'VE GOT NOTHING TO LOSE!
DM DM DM DM DM DM DM
...THAT I COULD DEFEAT RANMA!?
"STRONGEST IN THE WORLD" WOULD MEAN...

THE KIMEN SCHOOL OF MARTIAL ARTS CALLIGRAPHY ULTIMATE TECHNIQUE...!
FWA
FWA
FWA
THE MARK OF THE BATTLING GOD!
SHA!
TH--
THIS IS A-- !!

RYOGA, YOU JERK...!
CHIIIIIIRRUP
CHIII CHIII
HE CHALLENGES ME TO A FIGHT...
AIRMAIL
Ranma, Come to the vacant lot in the third district tomorrow at noon. —Ryoga Hibiki
HE'S A WEEK LATE NOW... NO SENSE OF DIRECTION AT ALL.
GETS LOST IN HIS OWN YARD.
HHSSHH
MYŌSHINKAN
DŌKAN
YŌKAN
DOJO
SHF
SHF
YOU JUST WALKED BY IT.
HEY...
SHF
SHF
WHERE'S THE VACANT LOT?

OKAY... THEN.
WHAT'S WITH ALL THOSE DOJO SIGNS?
FLOMP
ALONG THE WAY...
I CHALLENGED A FEW DOJOS...
MYOSH
WHOA...
I GUESS YOU MUST HAVE GOTTEN A BIT BETTER.
COME AT ME ANY WAY YOU LIKE, RANMA...
PRETTY CONFIDENT, AREN'TCHA?
OKAY THEN, HERE I COME!
TAH!
LET'S SEE WHAT YOU'VE GOT!
sSS

TAP
HUH
?
DONK
KRUMBL...
WHAT
THE...
?
WH--

WHAT'S THE MATTER, RANMA?
IF YOU DON'T COME AT ME SERIOUSLY, YOU'LL GET HURT.
YOU DON'T HAVE TO TELL ME TWICE...
HERE I COME!
SHP
VWIP
FLIP
FLIP
FLIP
NGH! NGH!
HE'S READING MY MOVES!
IMPOSSIBLE!
SHP
TAP

DWOOOOM
NNNGH!
I BEAT HIM...
...WITH ONLY MY PINKIE...
FARE-WELL, RANMA.
I'VE GOT NO USE FOR YOU NOW.
.....
DMF
I THOUGHT IF ANYONE...
...*YOU* COULD BE THE ONE WHO COULD BEAT ME.
SIGH...
RYOGA...?

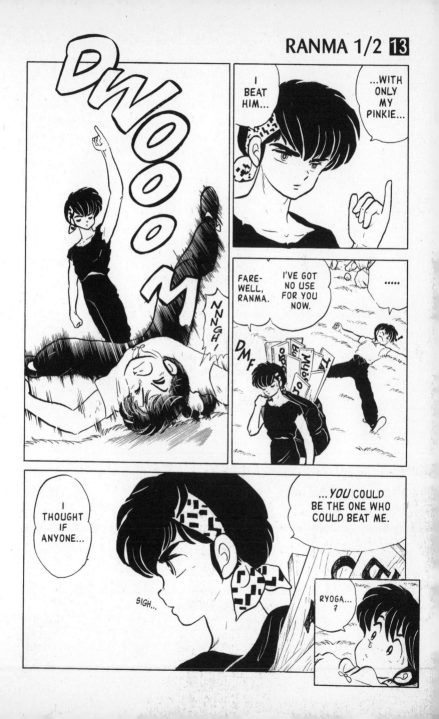

...MARTIAL ARTS CALLIGRAPHY?
UH-HUH.
WITH THE MARK OF THE BATTLING GOD UPON YOUR ABDOMEN, YOU'LL BECOME THE MOST POWERFUL MAN IN THE WORLD!
SHA!
AND WITH THE MARKINGS...
I DID BECOME THE STRONGEST MAN IN THE WORLD...
BUT AT THE SAME TIME...
...I'VE ALSO BECOME THE MOST TRAGIC MAN, AS WELL!
FWUP!!

HHSSHH
SHFF
SCRUB
SCRUB
SCRUB
SCRUB
SCRUB
SCRUB
IT'S USE-LESS...
...IT'S NOT SOMETHING YOU CAN JUST RUB OFF.
sigh
ffp
SCOUR SCOUR
SCOUR
SCOUR
SCOUR
THAT HURTS!
BWAK
I TRIED TO GET IT OFF MYSELF...
HHSSHH
...I TRIED PRACTICALLY EVERYTHING...

BUT...
HEY, OLD MAN!
GET THIS DOODLE OFF OF ME!
NOW!
THERE'S ONLY ONE WAY TO GET IT OFF.
THAT'S TO BE DEFEATED IN COMBAT.
THEN THE MARKINGS WILL DISAPPEAR ON THEIR OWN.
I SEE...
SO *THAT'S* WHY YOU'VE BEEN CHALLENGING ALL THESE DOJOS...
OF COURSE, I WON EVERY TIME...
LOOKS TO ME LIKE...
I'VE REACHED A LEVEL OF GREATNESS IN MY MARTIAL ARTS THAT YOU COULD NEVER HOPE TO ACHIEVE, RANMA.
FARE-WELL!
STOMP
--WAIT!

THAT MARKING...
I'LL GET RID OF IT FOR YOU!
LIKE I'VE TOLD YOU...
THE ONLY WAY FOR ME TO LOSE IT IS IN COMBAT.
SO, WHAT I'M TELLING YOU IS THAT I'LL BEAT YOU SOMEHOW!
.....
RYOGA... YOU'RE THE...
...ONLY MAN THAT I CONSIDER TO BE MY RIVAL.
!

AND YOU CAME TO ME, BECAUSE YOU NEEDED MY HELP, RIGHT!?
LEAVE IT TO ME!
ALL RIGHT !?
SIIIIIGH
RANMA...
YOU'RE...
SUCH A NICE GUY!
BWAK
HHSSHHHH
HM ?
RANMA...!
AFTER ALL THAT TALK...
HE RUNS AWAY!
I'LL...BEAT HIM...YOU... JUST... WATCH...!

PART 2
FACE OFF!

ALL RIGHT, RANMA. COME AT ME!
twee twee twee
天道道場
RYOGA... WHAT IN THE HELL...?
SHUT UP!
I HAVE TO LOSE TO YOU, REMEMBER?!

UNTIL I LOSE A FIGHT...
...I'LL NEVER BE ABLE TO RUB AWAY...
...THE FACE OF THE BATTLING GOD!
HUH.
AND YOU DON'T THINK I CAN BEAT YOU...
...UNLESS YOU'RE HANDICAPPED ?!
I'LL SHOW *YOU* WHAT --
DSH
RYEW
SMUNCH
DONK
...WELL, RANMA !?
I *SAID*, COME AT ME!
RRRRRRGH...
TWIK TWIK

JIIIIINNN
chirrup
chirrup
chirrup
TM TM TM TM TM TM TM TM
FWA FWA FWA
O-KAY!
THE SCROLL OF SECRET BLOWS!
FWA
CURSE YOU, RANMA.
IF I CAN'T COUNT ON YOU, WHO CAN I?
sigh

RYOGA!
EH?
HEH HEH HEH! PREPARE YOURSELF!
I'M NOT THE SAME OPPONENT I WAS A MINUTE AGO!
REALLY?!
ta!
THE SAOTOME DESPERATION STRIKE!!
D-D-DESP-P-PERATION... STRIKE...?!
WHAT... WHAT COULD IT...?

HEY !
WHAT'S THAT !?
FWIP
HUH ?
HE FELL FOR IT!
hsSh--
THE SECRET OF ATTACKING FROM BEHIND LIKE A HUNTING CANINE!
FOX-FU!!
SHA!
KLONG
SHKK
......
TWIK TWIK

OKAY...SAOTOME DESPERATION STRIKE #2!
FWA
STRIKING AN ENEMY TO THE GROUND WITH A SINGLE BLOW, LIKE A TIGER!
FELINE-FU!!
LOOK! A HUNDRED YEN!
WHERE ?! WHERE ?!
SHOOOMM
WHAT *IDIOT* WOULD FALL FOR *THAT?!*
GOSH
Oh! The old D.S.#2!

"DESPERATION STRIKE," MY STEELY BUTTOCKS!
I THOUGHT YOU WERE A FIGHTER!
TO SEE THE GREAT RANMA SAOTOME STOOPING TO CHEAP TRICKS, IT'S...
SOB
RANMA... ?
I'M... I'M SORRY RYOGA...
I'M JUST SO WEAK...
I CAN'T... S-S-SAVE YOU FROM YOUR CURSE...
I'M SO... SO... SORRRR-RRRRRY... !
BOO HOO HOO HOO
N-N-NO... ! RANMA...

DON'T BE SO HARD ON YOURSELF.
IT'S NOT YOUR FAULT.
I'VE JUST BECOME...
...TOO GOOD FOR YOU!
sigh
PWINK
SSSHHHH
WA-HA-HA! YOU FELL FOR IT!
THE ULTIMATE SAOTOME DESPERATION STRIKE...
B-KEEE!
BONK
...LULLING THE ENEMY INTO DROPPING HIS GUARD LIKE A TOAD IN THE ROAD!
FLAT-FROG-FU!!

...CAN'T BEAT A PIG!
AND THE DAY WILL NEVER DAWN WHEN I...
hhsSh
RRRR
sigh...
AAAAAH!
DWaooomm
P-CHAN!
hyoi

WHAT AWFUL PERSON...
WHAT HAPPENED TO YOU?! WHO DREW THIS?!
B-KEEE
...WOULD DOODLE SOMETHING...
...TO MAKE A POOR LITTLE PIG LOOK STUPID?!
STAB STAB
SIGH
KWEEE KWEEE
P-CHAN, WAIT!

SHE SAW IT...
MY AKANE... SAW IT...!
...LOOK STUPID...
...LOOK STUPID...!!
NOOOOOOOOOO
POOR IDIOT...
HEY, C'MON, MAN...
LISTEN...
I BEEN THINKIN'...

THAT DOODLE OF YOURS...IT'S NOT AS HOPELESS AS YOU THINK...
WHAT...?
HE KNOWS A WAY TO GET RID OF IT...HE'S ABOUT TO TELL ME...
FWA
WELCOME, New Employees!
BWA HA HA HA HA HA
HEY, EVERY-BODY!
GET A LOAD O' THIS!!
HOO HOO HA HA
YOU'RE A FUNNY GUY, RYOGA! I'M GLAD I HIRED YOU!
tee-hee!
he's so funny!
IT COULD BE GREAT AT PARTIES, Y'KNOW?
IS THAT... WHAT YOU CALL...
...THINKING?!
BOOM

P-CHAN, WHERE ARE YOU?!
LET ME WASH THAT STUPID DOODLE OFF!
HM ?
dok
WHONK
POOM!
...AKANE SAW THE MARK ON P-CHAN'S PIGGY TUMMY!
BECAUSE OF YOU... YOU...
GRRN GRRN GRRN
...EVER BE ABLE...
MEANING I'LL NEVER...
Sobb!

SO TELL ME WHY...
OH RIGHT.
VSH
...TO LET HER SEE MY STOMACH!
RYOGA... ?
...SHE'D WANT TO SEE YOUR STUPID STOMACH, ANYWAY!?
VWOP
...KANE... ?
A...

THE SAME DOODLE AS P-CHAN...?
SHK SHK SHK SHK SHK SHK
KROOM
THERE, THAT WASN'T SO BAD, WAS IT...?
EH-HEH-HEH-HEH
YOU... Y-Y-YOU...
WHAT'S GOING ON HERE...?

PART 3
THE MARK OF THE PIG

OWOOO
BOW
BOW
BOW
NO. I'M POSITIVE...
THE DOODLE ON P-CHAN...
...AND THE ONE ON RYOGA...
...WERE THE SAME...

OHHHH, RANMA...
BUT WHY ?!
fwip
LOOK IN A MIRROR.
WHY DO YOU KEEP TURNING AWAY FROM ME?
GWREE
fwip
THERE'S SOMETHING ABOUT P-CHAN...AND RYOGA...
HE HAS TO BE...
DON'T LET HER FIGURE IT OUT...
NO... PLEASE, NO...
B-BMP
B-BMP
B-BMP
B-BMP
D-DON'T BE STUPID.
...WHAT ARE YOU HIDING FROM ME?
GWREE
SHH

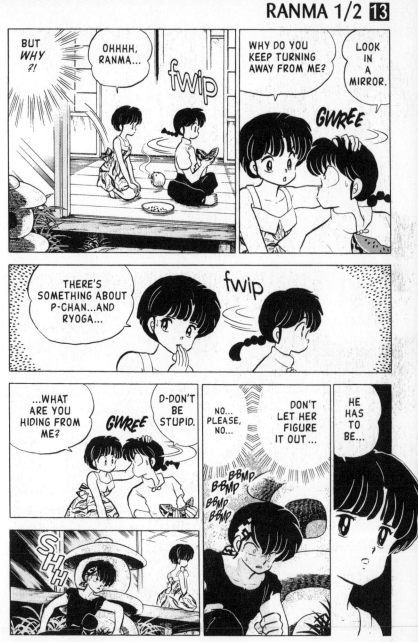

HE HAS TO BE *ONE* AND THE *SAME!*
BRRRRRRR
THE SAME PERSON DREW ON RYOGA AND P-CHAN!
.....
.....
AND...
--WHOA. HOLD IT.
I WON'T LET YOU SAY IT.
I MUST *CONFESS!*
SHWOP

WAY TO GO, SAOTOME !
WAY TO GO...
IT WAS ME!
ME...AND ME ALONE!
FWA
HOW DID I GET TO BE SO GOOD?
heh
I CAN'T BELIEVE I'M DOING THIS FOR THAT MORON...
THE DOODLE...
YOU FOOL !
BWOK
...WASN'T DRAWN THIS BADLY!

RYOGA...?
DEAREST AKANE...
AS LONG AS I HAVE THIS FACE ON MY BELLY...
...MY TERRIBLE SECRET MAY BE EXPOSED...
...I BID YOU...FARE-WELL.
HUH...?
YOU WHAT?
I LEAVE ON A QUEST!
SPOING
RYOGA?!

WHAT IS GOING ON HERE...?!
RANMA!
YOU ARE HIDING SOMETHING!
RANMA...?
FARE-WELL...
WHAT A MAROON...
...CRYING, NO LESS.
DOLT.
STILL...I CAN'T JUST LET HIM SUFFER...

I'VE GOT TO FIND A WAY TO *BEAT* THE POOR DOPE...
BUT RIGHT NOW, HE'S THE BEST FIGHTER THERE IS...:
EVEN DESPERATION STRIKES ARE USELESS...
THERE'S NO OPENING TO...
--OPENING ?!
THAT'S *IT!*
I'VE STILL GOT ONE CHANCE!
sha
tweee
twee
hff
hfff
hffff
shmp
shmp

SO... TIRED...
WALKED ALL NIGHT...BUT COULDN'T REST...
...KNOWING I'LL NEVER SEE MY AKANE AGAIN...
One-two! One-two!
.....
...Ryoga. How's it goin'
IT.... IT CAN'T BE!
gasp
I'VE WALKED BACK TO WHERE I ST-
RRRRRRRR
OH, PLEASE CATCH MY BALL FOR ME!
PYONG
EH?

HWA
AN OPENING !
WHAT -- ?!
BWUK
YES! I LANDED A...
POOOOM
...BLOW ?

WHO... WHAT...?
GNSH
Huh..?
M-MISS, ARE YOU...?
I WAS ONLY PL-PLAYING VOLLEYBALL... YOU DIDN'T HAVE T-TO *HIT* ME...!
WAAA
I'M... I'M SORRY.
WHEN ANYONE CHARGES ME, MY BODY JUST REACTS.
PLEASE FORGIVE ME.
HEH HEH HEH... THIS TIME HE'S WIDE OPEN...
SMIRK
BOW
boing
ELBOW...
HYAAA
...JAB?
BWOK

WHERE'D YOU GO?!
HEY!
I HIT A HELP-LESS LITTLE GIRL...TWICE!
GYAAAH!
HWRRRRR
BLOOSH
P-CHAN DISAPPEARED TOO...
WHEN RYOGA LEFT...
BUT WHAT DOES IT MEAN...?
IT'S STRANGE...
TM TM TM
CLINIC
Reasonable Rates
NO... NO...AND YET...
CAN IT BE...?

OH, P-CHAN!
I'M SO GLAD TO SEE YOU!
GYUU
UH...?
B-KEEEE
NOW THIS IS RIDICULOUS...
...BUT HOW...?!
...DID GET THROUGH HIS GUARD...
THAT ONE KICK...
--WAIT A SEC.
IT'S ONE THING TO HAVE GREAT REFLEXES...
...BUT IF YOU CAN'T EVEN LET A HIGH SCHOOL GIRL...

gasp
CAN IT BE... ?!
STOP SQUIRMING, P-CHAN!
I HAVE TO WASH THAT DOODLE OFF YOU.
SHKK SHKK
I STILL DON'T UNDERSTAND, THOUGH.
WHY WOULD YOU HAVE THE SAME DOODLE AS RYOGA?
I WISH YOU COULD TELL ME.
B-BMP B-BMP
GOSH, COULD IT BE...
SHKK
SHKK
SHKK
SHKK
Peneton

RYOGA'S OFF ON A QUEST AND YOU'RE HERE.
ISN'T THAT A SILLY IDEA?
NOD NOD
...THAT YOU'RE SECRETLY RYOGA?
KWEEE!
TIME TO WASH THE SOAP OFF...
...WITH SOME NICE HOT WATER!
DOOOOOM
BWEEEEK!

IF I'M RIGHT ABOUT THIS...
...WE CAN GET RID OF THAT FACE!
JUST HANG ON, RYOGA!
KLANK
KRRR...
P-CHAN... ?!
NO...
STAGGER...
Pen

PART 4

AKANE GUESSES THE SECRET!

I FIGURED OUT A WAY TO GET RID OF THAT *MARK!*
RYOGA! WHERE *ARE* YOU?!
SHTNG SHTNG
ERG.
HYUUUUUUUUUUU...
WHA-- ?!
SHTNG
RYOGA'S BANDANNA...
AND A KETTLE ?!
SHTNG
Peneton

AKANE
!
Y-Y-YOU DIDN'T POUR WATER ON... ON...ON...
SHE *DID* IT!
SHE KNOWS...
I WAS... I WAS...
...J-JUST TRYING TO WASH THAT DOODLE OFF P-CHAN'S ST-STOMACH AND...
MIIIINNN MIINN
CHRP CHRP CHRP CHRP
AH, RYOGA...
I'M SORRY, MAN...
LISTEN...
IT MUST'VE BEEN A SHOCK TO YOU, BUT...
DON'T BLAME RYOGA.
HE NEVER MEANT TO HURT YOU...

BUT... WHAT'S RYOGA...
...HAVE TO DO WITH IT?
NEEP ?
TIME TO WASH THE SOAP OFF WITH SOME NICE HOT WATER!
BWEEEK!
P-P-CHAN... NO!!
GLNK GLNK GLNK
GLNK GLNK
WHAT DOES RYOGA...
...HAVE TO DO WITH THAT?
gwi
.....

hsSh...

ZHEEE...
ZHEEE...

SLOSH
SLOSH

glg
glg
glg
glg

BWEEEK

Y'KNOW... YOU ARE ONE LUCKY MORON.

RANMA...

ARE YOU *SERIOUS?!* YOU CAN GET *RID* OF IT?!

YEAH. *IF MY THEORY IS CORRECT.*

MIIIINN

CHRP
CHRP
CHRP
CHRP
CHRP

OH, THERE YOU ARE, AKANE.
WHAT IS IT, KASUMI?
I WAS WONDERING IF YOU COULD HELP ME.
TODAY WE'RE...
ARE YOU SURE THIS IS GOING TO WORK?
tap tap
HEH. TALK ABOUT LUCKY!
WE CAN DO IT BEHIND THAT CURTAIN...
IT FINALLY HIT ME, AFTER FIGHTING YOU A COUPLE TIMES...
SHAA
...THAT WHILE YOU WERE STANDING...
...YOU NEVER HAD ONE TINY OPENING IN YOUR DEFENSE.

BUT ONCE...
...WHEN THAT INCREDIBLY GRACEFUL, BEAUTIFUL GIRL HIT A VOLLEYBALL TO YOU...
...AND YOU CROUCHED TO HIT IT BACK...
YOU WERE OPEN !
WHICH MEANS...
OF COURSE !
THAT GIRL WAS *YOU!*
MNKH
DOES THAT MATTER *NOW?!*
THEN WHAT ARE YOU *SAYING ?!*
THIS, IDIOT...
THAT WHEN YOU CROUCHED, YOU CHANGED THE SHAPE OF THE MARKING...
...AND THAT MEANS...

...IF I CAN CHANGE THIS THING'S EXPRESSION...
IT WON'T MAKE YOU INVULNER-ABLE.
AND THAT MEANS...
THEN THE MAGIC SHOULD FADE AWAY!
...I'LL BE ABLE TO BEAT YOU AS USUAL!
I SEE...
KWEE
.....
HSSH
KWEE
D-KONG

I THINK... YOU NEED... TO CHANGE IT...MORE...
I'M *TRYING*, BLAST YOU!
HOW ABOUT THIS ONE ?!
NOT GOOD ENOUGH !
KASUMI, ARE YOU READY YET?
ALMOST FINISHED, FATHER.
IT'S WEIRD...
WHAT WAS RANMA SO FREAKED ABOUT?
IT MUST'VE BEEN A SHOCK TO YOU, BUT...
...DON'T BLAME RYOGA.
WHAT IS IT... ?
WHAT'S GOING ON WITH RYOGA...?

ARRRGH! CAN'T YOU DO ANYTHING RIGHT?!
C'MON, STRETCH THAT THING!
MAKE LIKE AN OLD DRUNK WITH A BEER BELLY!
TWIST THAT STOMACH! TWIST! TWIST!
KREE KREE
NNNNRGH!
MORE! MORE!
NNGH!
WAHAHAHAHAHAHA!
WHAT'S SO FUNNY?!
THAT'S IT, FOOL!
YOU CAN DO IT!

STRIKE THE POSE!
THIS TIME I'M *CLOBBERING* YOU!
DON'T LET ME DOWN, RANMA! NOW...
NNNNNAAAGH!
B-BUMP B-BUMP
GNNYUUUU
SHAAAAAA

GASP
ULP.
KKK
HYUUUUUU
......

LADIES' CLUB
tee hee hee
YADA YAMA YADA
R... RYOGA...?
UM...
THE LADIES HAD TO RENT THE DOJO FOR THEIR MEETING...
WHO ARE THESE DAMES...?

WEE-HA!
WHICH ONE ?!
HOT STUFF THERE, SONNY!
HA HA HA HA HA HA HA
LOOK AT THAT STUPID FACE!
WHAT A MAROON !
TMP TMP
GO! GO! GO!
COME ON, BABY! SHAKE THAT THING!
HOO HOO HOO
I AM ONE...
BWA HA HA HA HA HA HA HA
FWEET FWEET FWEET
...UN-LUCKY MORON...
D-KONG

I WIN.
tweet tweet
FSSSSS...
LOOK! THE FACE IS VANISHING!
OOO!
A MAGIC SHOW!
THANK YOU VERY MUCH.
CLAP CLAP CLAP CLAP
FWEET FWEET
CLAP CLAP
CLAP CLAP
SO *THAT'S* THE SECRET!
tweet tweet
RYOGA WAS SECRETLY TRAINING TO ENTERTAIN THE *LADIES'* *CLUB!*

BUT WAIT A MINUTE...
chirrup chirrup chirrup
WHY DID P-CHAN HAVE THE SAME DOODLE AS RYOGA?
MAYBE RYOGA USED P-CHAN'S STOMACH FOR PRACTICE.
OH, THAT MAKES SENSE!
.....
AFTER ALL THE HELL RYOGA WENT THROUGH THIS TIME...
...HE'LL PROBABLY DISAPPEAR FOR A LONG WHILE...
OH! WELCOME BACK P-CHAN!
GONG
AND THE DOODLE IS GONE.
I'M SO GLAD.
BWII
SOMETIMES I THINK BEING STUPID CAN BE A MAJOR ADVANTAGE...

PART 5
SANTA'S LITTLE DISCIPLES

BYE-BYE!
SEE YOU TOMORROW!
BYE AKANE!
COME ON, HANAKO, WE'RE ALMOST THERE.
BUT I'M TOO TIRED.
HM?
CARROT
OH... WE'RE... UM...
WHAT'S WRONG?
CARROT
...LOOKING FOR THIS OLD MAN.

......
KILL KILL KILL KILL KILL KILL KILL
PANTY THIEF !
SHING SHING SHING
CARROT
YOO HOO, AKANE !
BYOING
WILL YOU QUIT BUGGIN' PEOPLE?!
BONK
EEEEE
YEEEEEE
DOMP BOMP
MUTTER MUTTER
HYUUUU
HMMMM...

WHAT DO YOU WANT WITH THIS HORRIBLE OLD MAN?
DID HE STEAL SOMETHING FROM YOU?
CARROT
HUH?
STEAL?!
SANTA DOESN'T STEAL!
WE FOUND HIM! WE FOUND SANTA!
Y...
YOU MEAN YOU'RE...
WE CAME TO SEE YOU! JUST LIKE WE PROMISED!
OKAY, HAPPOSAI...
...WHAT THE HECK IS THIS?!
AHEM
WELL ... THIS PAST CHRISTMAS EVE...
POING
POING
DECK THE HALLS WITH BRAS AND PANTIES...
...ON MY WAY HOME FROM MY NIGHTLY ROUNDS...

DO YOU WANT TO HAVE CHRISTMAS WITH ME?
AH, POOR DARLINGS...
POING
gwii
...I SAW A LONELY PAIR OF STOCKINGS, HUNG BY A WINDOW WITH CARE...
SHOOP
FWAP
TWONG
DONK
AN' HE BROUGHT ME SOME UNDIES!
WE CAUGHT SANTA CLAUS!
WE DID IT, HANAKO!
HOW COULD I DISILLUSION TWO INNOCENT TYKES?
PSS
PSS
...YOU WENT ALONG WITH IT?!
YOU MEAN...

AND WHEN THEY TOLD ME THEIR FATHER WAS OUT OF TOWN...
...AND THEIR MOTHER WOULDN'T BE HOME UNTIL LATE...
...I JUST FELT SO SORRY FOR THEM!
WOO HOO HOO HOO! MORE CHICKEN!
MORE CAKE! MORE SAKE!!
ALL I WANTED WAS TO BRING THEM CHRISTMAS CHEER.
UH HUH. TELL ME ANOTHER ONE.
MURRAY KISHMASH...
...'N T'WALL A G'NIGH.
pik pik
SANTA, WAIT!
I WANT TO BE YOUR HELPER WHEN I GROW UP.
CAN'T YOU TEACH ME HOW?
BWAHAHAHAHA! COME SEE ME ANYTIME AN' I'LL MAKE YOU MY DISCIPLE!
I WILL, I WILL!
BWUH

O-KAY... AND NOW...?
I DIDN'T THINK THEY'D ACTUALLY FIND ME!
BUT SANTA, ON THE PRESENT YOU GAVE US...
.....
NERIMA'S TENDO DOJO
YOU WRITE YOUR *ADDRESS*...ON YOUR *STOLEN* UNDERWEAR?!
bonk
YOU PROMISED, SANTA! MAKE ME YOUR DISCIPLE!
I'LL DO ANYTHING! I DON'T CARE HOW HARD IT IS!
WHAT DO YOU PLAN TO DO?
RRRRM... MUMBLE MUMBLE MUMBLE...
ALL RIGHT, ALL RIGHT.
NEVER SAY I BROKE A PROMISE!
wap
FOLLOW ME!
YOUR TRAINING STARTS NOW!
YES, SIR!
TM TM TM TM

THE FIRST RULE OF SANTAHOOD!
NEVER LET YOURSELF BE SEEN!
YES SIR !
SNEAK
FWIP
FWIP FWIP
HEY.
WHAT'RE YOU PULLING ?
WE'RE GATHERING PRESENTS, OF COURSE!
WOOMP
MERRY CHRISTMAS !
STF STF STF
HOLD IT, YOU--

SHOOP
urk
DOKONG
SECOND RULE!
KNOW YOUR WAY AROUND CHIMNEYS!
BATH HOUSE
BLOOSH
HSSSSH
SPLASH
BGGYNNG
STOP RIGHT THERE.
YOU AGAIN!
NO PRESENTS FOR YOU THIS YEAR, YOUNG MAN!
JUST WHAT DO YOU THINK YOU'RE TEACHING THESE KIDS?!

NOW LISTEN, KIDS...
IF YOU THINK THIS IS REALLY SANTA, YOU NEED TO LEARN A FEW--
WAK !
HAVE YOU NO RESPECT FOR INNOCENCE ?!
TONG
IT'S NOT WHAT IT LOOKS LIKE!
EEEEEEEEEEEEEEEEEE...
FEH.
AMATEURS...
eeek
eeek
BONNK
DONK
THE THIRD LAW!
BE QUICK ON YOUR FEET!
RAMEN
GLMP GLMP GLMP GLMP GLMP GLMP GLMP

PARTICULARLY...
pik pik
...AFTER EATING !!
VSSH
STOP! THE CHECK !
THERE'S NO BETTER WAY TO BUILD STRONG LEGS AND LOSE...
EH ?
HYUUUUUUU
RAMEN
STATIONERY
Cafe
PAWN SHOP
Ramen
DO YOU THINK...
MAYBE SANTA'S POOR ?
YEAH...
GCHAKK
KSSHH
.....
ONE TWO THREE
IS IT ENOUGH ?
CHK CHK
HE MUST BE USING ALL HIS MONEY...
...TO BUY PRESENTS FOR OTHERS.
RATTLE

RRRRRGH!!
THAT... SICK... OLD... FREAK...
SHF-KLMP SHF-KLMP
HUH?
WHAT'S THE FOURTH RULE, SANTA?
TWINKLE TWINKLE
NGH!
SUCH... INNOCENCE...
EVERY DISCIPLE I'VE EVER HAD...
...HAS TREATED ME WITH SUCH DIS-RESPECT...
...UNTIL NOW...
THIS IS THE FIRST TIME...
...I'VE EVER BEEN TRULY UNDERSTOOD... AND TREATED WITH THE KINDNESS I DESERVE!

GYURRNG
TRUST ME. YOU NEVER GOT *HALF* WHAT YOU DESERVE!
.....
OH, PLEASE, SIR! STOP HURTING SANTA CLAUS!
PAP PAP
IS THERE ANY CONSCIENCE IN THERE AT ALL?
FEH...
THE FOURTH LAW!
DO GOOD *DEEDS* !!
GRRRRRR
I'LL SHOW YOU CONSCIENCE !
WHAT KINDA GOOD DEEDS, SANTA?!
TWINKLE TWINKLE
GOOD DEEDS...
UM... YES...
GOOD DEEDS...
GNYEE
GOO... GOO... GOO-WOOO...

BOOM
SHORTED HIMSELF OUT, EH?
HE FINALLY WENT TOO FAR...
WE'RE LUCKY HE DIDN'T TRY TO DO A GOOD DEED...
HE MIGHT HAVE BLOWN US ALL UP.
OOOG NNNNGH URRRGLE
POOR SANTA...
YOU NEVER HAD ALL THIS TROUBLE...
...'TIL YOU TRIED TEACHING US...
WE'VE LEARNED OUR LESSON.
WE GIVE UP BEING YOUR DISCIPLES.
UH...?
OH, BUT...
WE BROUGHT YOU A PRESENT...
IT'S IN HERE...

WE KNOW YOU LOVE UNDER-WEAR, SO...
P-P-PANTIES!
PING
IT'S A MIRACLE!
POING
I HOPE THEY'RE NOT TOO BIG.
THEY'RE MY DAD'S...
BOOM
THE FINAL BLOW...
EVEN HE HAS HIS LIMITS...
SSS...
WE HOPE YOU GET BETTER SOON!
I DIDN'T KNOW IT WOULD BE SO HARD.
I GUESS I'LL NEVER GET TO BE SANTA'S HELPER.
BUT YOU CAN STILL DO GOOD DEEDS.
YOU SURE CAN.
EVEN BETTER THAN *SANTA* WAS DOING!
DON'T YOU THINK EVEN HAPPOSAI HAS TO FEEL JUST A *LITTLE* BAD ABOUT THIS?
I WOULDN'T COUNT ON IT.

HUH ?
HYURURURU
LOOKA ME!
IT'S A SANTA FIRE-BURST !
PAP
BE GOOD, CHILDREN !
AND YOUR STOCKINGS WILL BE FULL THIS YEAR!
POOOOOOM
OH SANTA... !
YOU SEE? HE CAN DO A GOOD DEED!
YEAH, WELL... I'LL WAIT TO SEE WHAT HE FILLS THOSE STOCKINGS WITH...

PART 6
WHEN YOU WISH UPON A SWORD

SPECIAL DELIVERY!
FOR AKANE TENDO AND... "THE PIGTAILED GIRL"?!
FOR ME AND RANMA...?
WHO'S IT FROM?
RRIP RRIP
WHO ELSE WOULD ADDRESS IT TO "THE PIG-TAILED GIRL"?! KUNO!
IT'S HEAVY...
fmp
RIP RIP
HUH?

HHHHHH...
AKANE TENDO...
PIGTAILED GIRL...
I WILL BE UNABLE TO ATTEND SCHOOL FOR THE NEXT THREE DAYS, DUE TO... PERSONAL REASONS. HEH HEH.
VNNNNNNN...
SOMETIMES I WISH BAD TASTE WAS A *CRIME*.
ZH ZH
YOU WILL BE LONELY, I KNOW.
THAT IS WHY I SEND YOU THIS STATUE...
...THAT YOU MAY GAZE LOVINGLY UPON IT UNTIL I RETURN TO Y-
FZZT
GOMP

GONNNNG
WAIT IN LINE, GENTLEMEN!
I'M SURE YOU'LL ALL HAVE A CHANCE TO TRY DRAWING OUT THE *WISH-BRINGER*.
MRMR MRMR
GRMBL GRMBL
BAH. WHAT FOOLS THEY ARE...
...GATHERING HERE ON THIS DAY EVERY YEAR, HOPING TO MAKE THE SACRED BLADE THEIR OWN.

...IT WILL GRANT ITS LIBERATOR THREE WISHES!
...THAT WHEN FINALLY DRAWN...
...TRAPPED WITHIN ITS STONE, TANTALIZING WITH ITS SHINING PROMISE...
AND YET, SINCE FEUDAL DAYS IT HAS SAT...
...ONLY TO FIND THEMSELVES UNEQUAL TO THE TASK.
THE GREATEST WARRIORS OF HISTORY HAVE TRIED...
NOT TODAY, YOUNG MAN! HO HO HO.
NKH NKH NKH NKH NKH NKH.
MRMR
MRMR
AND NOW, THESE MODERN WEAKLINGS...

NO STRENGTH OR SKILL CAN FREE THE WISHBRINGER.
IT WILL SLIP FREE *ONLY* WHEN GRASPED...
...BY THE ONE *DESTINED* TO OWN IT!
NNNN-NNNG-YARH!!
THANK YOU. NEXT!
HNNN-GWU-HH!!
CAW CAW
LOVELY. NEXT !
TMP
NEX...
OH!
M-M-MASTER... IF THE PR-PROPHECIES ARE *TRUE*, TH-THEN...
IS IT POSSIBLE... ?

ACCORDING TO THIS SCROLL PASSED DOWN THROUGH THE AGES...
YES! THERE IS NO DOUBT!
HE IS THE WISHBRINGER'S CHOSEN!
THIS MAN IS HE!
SHHHHH
OOOH!
...MY DESTINY ?!
GNG
C-CAN THIS TRULY BE...
YADA YADA

IT IS DONE!
THE WISH-BRINGER HAS BEEN CLAIMED AT LAST!
CAW CAW
ARK ARK
CAW CAW
A SACRED BLADE THAT GRANTS THREE WISHES...
THREE... WISHES...
HMMM...
THIS IS A PROBLEM.
AFTER ALL...
I'M GORGEOUS! I'M BRILLIANT! I'M RICH!
I EVEN HAVE A GREAT PERSONALITY!
WHAT AM I GOING TO DO WITH THREE WISHES?!
PSS PSS
Let's go around...

HUMBLE THIS FOOL !
YOUR WISH IS MY COMMAND.
gasp
HEH...
SO WHERE WERE YA?
HEY KUNO, WELCOME BACK!
MNSH
SHK
NUMBER ONE !
WISH-BRINGER !
A REAL SWORD !
EEK !

THE SWORD... IT TALKED!
HUH? IZZAT KUNO?
AND RANMA...
FOR RENT
PREPARE YOURSELF!
HYAAAAA
HEH.
EEEEEE!
YOU THINK I'M AFRAID OF SOME CHEAP SWORD?!
SHA
BWONG
WHA?!
AN OPENING!
DOMMM!

IT IS DONE...
TA-DAAA
ARE YOU OKAY, RANMA?
BWOOP
NNNNGH...
NOW YOU KNOW...
...NEVER TO CHALLENGE MY PROWESS AGAIN.
ching
THAT SWORD...
...WHAT WAS IT?
MRMR MRMR
HMM...
POST NO BEARS
Correct me if I'm wrong...
...but that looks like the Wishbringer!

THE ONE MAN DESTINED TO DRAW IT?
YOU?
THERE MUST BE SOME MISTAKE.
FEH. IF YOU DON'T BELIEVE ME...
TAKE A LOOK AT THIS ANCIENT SCROLL.
fwip
THE PRIESTS READ IT ...AND KNEW I WAS THE ONE!
FWA
WH-WHAT THE...?
.....
WHAT IS THIS?
WELL...

CONGRATULATIONS! YOU'RE OUR ONE MILLIONTH SWORD-PULLER!
CLAP CLAP CLAP CLAP
CLAP CLAP CLAP
tik
AARGH! OF ALL THE LUCK!
BAH!
I SHALL NEVER FORGET THAT FEELING OF... PRIDE!
SOBB
WELL...
I GUESS IT'S LIKE WINNING THE LOTTERY.
OKAY, SO HOWEVER HE GOT IT...
...HE'S STILL GOT TWO WISHES LEFT, RIGHT?
HEH...

WITH THE POWER OF THE WISH-BRINGER...
NYAH HAH—HAH HAH HAH HAH HAH
...I CAN TAKE OVER THE *WORLD!*
AAAAAA!
WE GOTTA GET THAT SWORD AWAY FROM HIM!
MY SECOND WISH IS CLEAR...
SHK
I WISH TO DATE THE *PIGTAILED GIRL!*
BOOOOM
YOUR WISH IS MY COMMAND.
THANK GOD...
YEAH... THANK GOD HE'S AN IDIOT...
WHEW...

A SWORD THAT GRANTS WISHES?!
NO KIDDING, POPS?
NO KIDDING.
NOW LISTEN...
IF WE GET THAT SWORD... WE GET THOSE WISHES!
TH-THEN... THAT WOULD MEAN...
I'D NEVER HAVE TO BE A GIRL AGAIN!
I'D NEVER HAVE TO BE A PANDA AGAIN!
SHOOOOOM

sponk
HUH?
A MESSAGE?
My beloved Kuno,
Please, please won't you ask me out again?
Forever yours,
The Pigtailed Girl.
BLAM
WAAAH!! ALREADY?!
WISH-BRINGER, I LOVE YOU!
POP
HEH HEH HEH...ENJOY IT WHILE YOU CAN, FOOL!

PART 7
MAY I CUT IN?

YOU CAN'T BE SERIOUS!
GOING OUT... WITH KUNO?!
THAT MAGIC SWORD HE'S GOT...
...CAME OUT OF THE ROCK WITH THREE WISHES IN IT!
FROM WHAT I HEAR...
KUNO'S ALREADY USED TWO OF THOSE...
WHICH MEANS YOU'VE GOT TO GET IT QUICKLY...BEFORE HE USES THE LAST WISH!
RELAX, POPS. IT'S A DONE DEAL.
FOR THE CHANCE TO BE ALL-MALE, ALL THE TIME...
HECK, I'LL EVEN...
GRNCH

...BE THE PRETTIEST LI'L THING YOU EVER SAW!
Teeheeheeheehee
THAT'S MY BOY!
.....
THE CAFE!
THE MOVIES!
THE FAIR!
I'LL HAVE ALL THE CHANCES I NEED!

PFF.
RANMA, YOU ARE SO NAIVE.
NABIKI...?
YOU THINK A DATE WITH KUNO...
...IS GONNA GO THAT SMOOTHLY?
TRUE... IT IS KUNO...
BWOOOO
OH, SHOOT! WE MISSED THE LAST TRAIN.
GEE, I'M A LITTLE TIPSY!
HERE.
THIS WILL TAKE CARE OF YOU!
SHA
KNOCKOUT DROPS
SHF SHF

fmp
NYAHAHAHAHA! SO, YOU WANT THE WISHBRINGER, DO YOU?!
RRRRRIP
EEEEK!
BRRRRR! THE HORROR!
HEY.
LEAVE ME OUTTA YOUR SICK FANTASIES, OKAY?
OH, RANMA... POOR RANMA...
YOU NEED LIPSTICK.
SO, YOU THINK A MINI-SKIRT IS BETTER?

twee twee
tk tk tk
SHNAWW
GRSNX
TM TM TM TM TM TM TM
TOOM
GOOD MORNING, PIGTAILED GIRL!
ZHOOP
LET US BE OFF!
GNAH?

DN DN DN DN DN DN
WHAT IS IT ?!
IT MUST BE A THIEF!
WHA
WHA
WHA...
HA HA HA! WHO'S A LITTLE SLEEPY-HEAD, HM?
TUNK
DO YOU HAVE ANY IDEA... WHAT TIME IT IS?
MNSH
KUNO ?!
WH... WHAT... ?
AH! DEAREST AKANE!
FORGIVE ME.
FOR TODAY... I BELONG TO THE PIG-TAILED GIRL.

BUT FEAR NOT, AKANE TENDO!
SHF
FOR MY FINAL WISH...
ping
NO NO NO NO NO NO!!
...I'LL WISH FOR A DATE WITH Y--
MONK
I'M READY! WHATCHA WAITIN' FOR?
SHHHH...
NAMAN DAMA NAMAN DAMA
AH!
HOW GRAND TO WITNESS THE BIRTH OF A NEW DAY!
OOOO, SO PRETTY!

HO HOHO HOHO !
YOU'RE FALLING BEHIND, PIGTAILED GIRL!
ZHAA
ZHAA
BUT KUNO, YOU RUN SO FAST! TEE HEE!
ZHAA
ZHAA
EEK !
SHWUMP
PIG-TAILED GIRL...
ARE YOU ALL RIGHT!?
SHMP
GOTCHA GOTCHA GOTCHA!
TEE HEE HEE!
SKWEEZ
OH...P-PIGTAILED GIRL...
HSS
THAT SWORD...IS MINE!!

GWOM
NOW, NOW, NOW, MY LITTLE PIG-TAILED PRETTY!
A LADY SHOULDN'T BE SO FORWARD!
AAA!
AAA!
fmp...
MY DIARY
A TRUE RELATIONSHIP IS BASED ON SHARED INTIMACIES! PLEASE... READ MY DIARY!
HOO HOO HOO
OH, KUNO... YOU'RE S-S-SUCH A G-GENTLE-MAN...
NOW WE WILL HAVE LUNCH!
ISN'T IT DELICIOUS?
I MADE IT ALL MYSELF!
HO HO HO
OH, KUNO, YOU'RE WONDERFUL!
THANKS FOR THE TIP, AKANE!
SHA
KNOCKOUT DROPS

SHF
SHF
SAY "AHHH."
GLOP
I...I HOPE...
...THAT WASN'T TOO FORWARD OF ME...
BLUSH
SHNAWW
EH ?
TAKING A NAP !
HOW SWEET !
YES.
AND SO HEALTHY, TOO.
HHSSHHHHHHHHHH

GONG
AND THIS ISN'T "FORWARD" ?!
OF COURSE...
ONE L-L-L-LITTLE K-K-K-KISS W-WON'T HURT ANY...
HWAH ?
SPLASH
WHAT DO YOU THINK YOU'RE DOING!?
RANMA !
GWAAAAAAH!!
IT'S MINE! MINE!
VROOM
COME BACK HERE, YOU CROOK!

WAIT! PLEASE! YOU MUSTN'T BE AFRAID!
FOOM
GYUU
ACK!
I GOT NEWS FOR YOU, KUNO...
I'M NOT !!
BOOT
WISH-BRINGER... I COMMAND YOU...
SHHH
NO.
...FREE ME OF THE PANDA!
KRAK

BZZT.
VOICE CHECK NOT VERIFIED.
YOUR WISH IS INVALID.
AH-HAH!
SO THE ONLY ONE IT GRANTS WISHES TO IS ITS *OWNER*!
WHAT?!
TH-THEN THAT MEANS...
DNK
ALL I HAVE TO DO IS ASK MY DARLING KUNO TO MAKE THE WISH *FOR* ME!
tee hee
......
HERE, KUNO! I BROUGHT BACK YOUR LI'L SWORDIE-SWORD!
AH, THANK YOU!
BOO HOO HOO
MAYBE I *DO* HAVE SOMETHING TO WORRY ABOUT AFTER ALL...

PART 8
THE FINAL WISH

COME BACK HERE, YOU!
HAHA-HAHA-HA!
TEE-HEE HEE! CATCH ME IF YOU CA-A-A-AN!
FIRST THE BEACH... NOW THE MOUNTAINS...
I GUESS KUNO'S THE OUTDOORSY TYPE.
I WANT YOU TO WISH AWAY A FEMININE PROBLEM OF MINE!
I SHALL HAVE THE *WISHBRINGER* MAKE IT SO!
BUT STILL...
...I CAN'T BELIEVE EVEN *RANMA* COULD PULL THIS OFF!
I *DON'T* THINK IT'LL BE THAT EASY...

YOU JUST WATCH! WITH MY *FEMININE WILES*...
...I'LL HAVE HIM *BEGGIN'* TO USE THAT WISH ON ME!
COME HERE, YOU!
HUHH HUHH
EEEK!
Y-YOU'RE SO... FAST!
ZHEE ZHEE
EEEK!
ALL RIGHT!
HSSH
I'LL WISH THAT I CAN CATCH YOU!
BWOK
DON'T BE WASTING THE WISH ON *IDIOCY*... *IDIOT*!

HAHAHA! I'M ONLY KIDDING.
OH, YOU SILLY!
tee hee
SAY, YOU ONLY HAVE ONE WISH LEFT, RIGHT?
YOU SHOULD SAVE IT FOR SOMETHING IMPORTANT.
BUT OF COURSE!
YOU MUST BE TIRED FROM ALL THAT RUNNING!
I'LL HAVE THE MAGIC SWORD BRING US A CAFE!
HSS
H
DON'T YOU DARE!!
Tweet
SSHH
WHAT?! A PROBLEM, YOU SAY?!
CHR CHR
VISTA POINT

I'M SURE I CAN HELP!
REALLY?
I AM A MAN OF MY WORD!
IT'S A PROMISE, THEN!
W-WELL...
IT'S ABOUT MY BODY...
sigh
REALLY?
I THINK YOU'RE FINE JUST AS YOU ARE.
OGLE OGLE
BUT IF YOU SAY SO...
I DO!
HSS
H
WISHBRINGER... BRING THE PIGTAILED GIRL BIGGER B--
THAT'S NOT *IT!!*

RANMA TALKED BIG...BUT IT'S *KUNO* WHO'S CALLING THE SHOTS!
NOW LET US GO AND FIND SOME LUNCH!
HAHAHA, ISN'T THIS FUN?
SSSH
Bed & Breakfast
HERE YOU ARE!
SAY *"AHH..."*
AHHH...
.....
THIS IS SO LAME...
I DON'T KNOW HOW MUCH LONGER I CAN HOLD OUT, IF I DON'T GET SOME RESULTS...

P-
PIGTAILED
GIRL...!
OH,
KU-
U-
UNO...
PRRR
PRRR
I DIDN'T WANNA
HAVE TO RESORT TO
THIS...BUT I GOTTA
START LAYING ON
THE CHARM!
IF YOU USE
THAT LI'L OL'
SWORD ON
MY WISH...
WHAT'S
HE
DOING...?
WHAT--
?
"A-A-A-A-
N-N-NY-
TH-THING"?!
B-BMP B-BMP
B-BMP
I'LL DO
ANNNY-THING
YOU WANT
ME TO!
B-BOOOM

GWAAAP
YOU SADDEN YOUR FATHER, BOY...
boo hoo
HAVE YOU NO *SHAME* ?!
RANMA !
SHE IS SO JEALOUS OF THE PIG-TAILED GIRL...
SIGH
SHE CAME ALL THIS WAY AFTER ME...
WHAT'S *SHE* GOT TO DO WITH IT?!
AKA-KA-KANE... TEN-ENDO...
YOU *WISH* !
MNSH
SO IN *LOVE* WITH ME!
ARE YOU *THAT* DESPERATE TO STOP BEING A GIRL?!
STAY *OUTTA* THIS, AKANE!
GET *BACK* HERE!
FORGIVE ME, AKANE TENDO!
TMP TMP TMP TMP
COME *ON*, KUNO !
YOU DON'T KNOW THE HALF OF IT!

RAN-
MAA
!!
TM
TM
TM
TM
I CAN HIDE IN THAT WATERFALL...
PSH
PSH
PSH
PSH
.....
WE'RE SAFE IN HERE, KUNO.
I LOST THEM...
ERG...
PSH
PSH
PSH
PSH
HEH HEH
WORLD-FAMOUS
HOT-WATER FALLS

HRRRRRRR
R-R-RANMA... SAO...TO... ME...!
HUH ?
OH... BOY OH BOY...
WHERE... DID YOU HIDE...
...THE PIGTAILED GIRL!!
VWOOP
VWOOP
WAIT... OF COURSE !
WHAT COULD MATTER MORE...
WISHBRINGER! FIND ME THE PIGTAILED--
BONK
FIRE
BCOSH
SILLY! YOU DON'T NEED A WISH FOR THAT!
CANDIES
SOUVENIRS

OH, PIGTAILED GIRL, HOW I'VE MISSED YOU!
HNSH
OH... KUNO!
I'VE ALMOST GOT HIM...
AB-B-BOUT WHAT YOU SAID...
ANYTHING, KUNO!
I'LL DO IT!
TH-TH-THEN...
CL-CLOSE YOUR EYES...

OUR FIRST DATE... OUR FIRST KISS...
SIGH
OH, HOW LUCKY I AM!
HEH HEH HEH...
PAP PAP
IF YOU WANT IT THAT BADLY...
I WON'T STOP YOU.
GO AHEAD AND *K-KISS* HIM!
YOU HAVE YOUR F-FATHER'S BL-BL-BLESSING!
DID I *ASK* FOR IT ?!
YEAH. GO AHEAD.
I WON'T STOP YOU EITHER.
AKA-KANE TENDO !
DON'T WORRY !
I'LL BE HAPPY TO KISS YOU SOON AS I'M THROUGH KISSING--
DON'T *BOTHER* !

ZHA
ONE MOMENT OF HORROR...
THAT'S ALL...
...AND I'LL BE A MAN AGAIN!!
GWEE
OH, RANMA... YOU FOOL!

AAAUGH! I CAN'T *DO* IT!
DOKLONG
RANMA...?
I JUST... PLAIN... *CAN'T!*
THIS DATE...
OWEE...
ZZHH
...IS NOW *OVER*!!
HWIP
BORP BORP
HOLD, PIG-TAILED GIRL!
I TRULY... *TRULY*...
...ENJOYED OUR DATE TODAY.
HUH...?

FROM THE BEGINNING, I HAD INTENDED TO GIVE YOU THE FINAL WISH AS A GIFT...
heh
VWII
NOW COMES THE FINAL WISH!
WISH-BRINGER!
YOU... YOU INTENDED...
YOU WHAT?!
HOW COULD I MISJUDGE HIM?
OH, KUNO...

YOUR WISH IS MY COMMAND.
BLAAAAM!
IN MEMORY OF THE FIRST DATE OF TATEWAKI KUNO AND THE PIGTAILED GIRL
WELL, IT *IS* A LOVELY LITTLE STATUE...
KUNO SAID HE COULD TELL JUST WHAT THE PIGTAILED GIRL WANTED MOST...
THIS IS WHAT YOU WANTED, RANMA?
NOOOOO!!!
BETTER THAN I EVER GOT.

PART 9
THE KING IS WILD

FWSH
OKONOMIYAKI
Ucchan's
CLOSED
CLOSED
SH SH
OKAY-- ANOTHER DAY AT THE SALT MINES.
KWRR
OPEN
SHMM
EH ?
DANGER ?!
WHO'S THERE !?
SHAA

PSH
PSH
FSSSHH
PLAYING CARDS ?
EH ?
WHAT ARE YOU SAYING ?!
VOO
YOU LOSE, UKYO...
HEH HEH HEH...
A ROYAL FLUSH !!
VWA
THIS !
WHEREAS I HOLD...
YOU HAVE ONLY A PAIR.
SHF

GOOD FOR YOU.
NOW WHO IN HECK *ARE* YOU?!
MONG...
RRRRRR...
YOU...
YOU'RE... YOU'RE...
THE GAMBLING KING?! HE'S BACK?!
"GAMBLING KING"... ?

Artist's Impression
SO HE IS KNOWN...
...FOR WHEN IT COMES TO GAMES OF CHANCE...
...HE IS SAID TO BE UNBEATABLE!!
WHY WOULD RANMA KNOW A GAMBLER...?
IT'S ABOUT THAT DEBT FROM TEN YEARS AGO...
HE'S COME BACK...
...TO PAY US BACK FOR WHAT WE DID!!
HWYU
SNAKE-EYE!

ZONG
AND A BOXCAR FOR YOU, RANMA... HEH HEH HEH!
FIP
YOU SHOULD HAVE KNOWN BETTER...
...THAN TO TRY YOUR LUCK AGAINST THE GAMBLING KING!
VWAA
御守

FOR TEN YEARS... 520 WEEKS... 3,653 DAYS...
...I HAVE WAITED TO DEFEAT YOU.
YOU SHOULD FEEL HONORED!
I CAN'T BEGIN TO TELL YOU...
MNSH
WHAT COULD HAVE HAPPENED BETWEEN THEM...
...WHEN RANMA WAS SO YOUNG...?

TEN YEARS AGO...
いろは
WHEE-WHEE
AUTUMN FESTIVAL
...I WAS RUNNING MY BUSINESS AS USUAL...
YOU LOSE!
RRG
...WHEN...
WAIT JUST A MINUTE!
FWEE
ARE YOU THE ONE WHO'S BEEN TAKING ALL THESE KIDS' MONEY?
HOW 'BOUT IT?
YOU AND ME...ONE-ON-ONE?
I ACCEPT.
THE GAME?

OLD MAID !!
I FELT NO FEAR. OLD MAID WAS THE FIRST GAME I'D MASTERED.
YOU LOSE !
AAAK !!
ONE MORE GAME!
YOU LOSE.
ONE MORE !
YOU LOSE !
AND THEN... ?
HA HA HA HA...
IT WAS MY SWEETEST VICTORY!
Entitles Bearer to ownership of my Okonomiyaki cart. Signed, Ukyo Kuonji
I'D LOST MY DAD'S FAST -FOOD BUSINESS TO HIM...SO...
RAN-CHAN! GET HIM FOR ME!
NO PROBLEM.

GAMBLING KING! PREPARE TO MEET YOUR MATCH!
POPCORN
AAAK !!
YOU LOSE.
ONE MORE GAME !
YOU LOSE.
ONE MORE !
YOU LOSE.
EEE-YAARG !
BONNNG
FOOLISH CHILD.
YOU HAVE NOTHING LEFT TO WAGER.
YES I DO!
HERE'S THE DEED!
VWA
VERY GENEROUS OF YOU.

AT THAT POINT...
...FINDING MYSELF AT THE END OF MY ROPE...
WE WRAPPED HIM UP LIKE SUSHI AND DUMPED HIM IN THE RIVER.
YOU... WHAT?!
NO *WONDER* HE HATES YOU SO MUCH!
YOU SEE?! I'M THE *VICTIM* HERE!
OH. THE "VICTIM," EH...?
LOOK! HE DROPPED HIS CARDS!
WAIT A SECOND...
THEY'RE ALL *JOKERS*!
HE WAS *CHEATING*!

WHAT KINDA "VICTIM" CHEATS LITTLE KIDS OUT OF THEIR MONEY?!
FEH...
MNSH
HAVE YOU FORGOTTEN ?
I STILL HOLD THE PAPERS!
SMIRK
I HEARD THE WHOLE STORY.
DAD...?
YIP
IF YOU MADE AN AGREEMENT, YOU MUST LIVE UP TO IT.
RANMA...
HAND OVER WHATEVER YOU PROMISED HIM
...AND HAVE HIM GO ON HIS WAY.
HEY, JUST BECAUSE IT'S NO SKIN OFF YOUR NOSE...
HUH ?
Entitles Bearer to ownership of my Okonomiyaki cart.
Signed, Ukyo Kuonji
COME TO THINK OF IT...

THE OKONOMIYAKI CART WAS RIPPED OFF BY RAN-CHAN'S *OLD MAN!*
LA LA LA...
YOU MEAN...
YOU DON'T HAVE IT ANYMORE?
WELL... IN ANY CASE...
RUSTLE RUSTLE
...I CAN AT LEAST COLLECT WHAT RANMA LOST TO ME.
RANMA?
WHAT DID YOU HAVE TO BET?
HMM... WHAT WAS IT...?
I WAS STILL A KID BACK THEN, SO...
HA HA HA
IT'S BOUND TO BE SOME WORTHLESS LITTLE THING, ISN'T IT?

FWA
AS WE AGREED...
...I WILL TAKE THE TENDO DOJO!
Entitles the Bearer to ownership of the Tendo Dojo.
Signed,
Ranma Saotome
KRUKKLE
HEH HEH HEH HEH HEH...
OOBOO WOOOOOO

BUT WHAT *IS* A TENDO DOJO?
A MARTIAL ARTS SCHOOL THAT BELONGS TO MY POP'S FRIEND.
IT'S NOT MINE YET...
BUT SOME-DAY...IT *WILL* BE!
RANMA... YOU ARE SO...
I NEVER SAID ANY-THING OF THE...
RAAAAN-MAAAA...
YEEE...
I REMEMBER HEARING IT MYSELF!
SURE YOU DID, RANMA, HONEY!
WELL, IT'S A LEGAL DOCUMENT...
UM...
HSST...
HYUUU
いろは
GOOD NIGHT!
I'LL BE BACK TOMORROW TO MOVE IN. PLEASE BE READY TO MORE OUT.

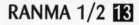

...SO YOU GO GET IT BACK!!!
K-BOOOOM
RANMA...
BOW WOW WOW WOW
BLAST THAT GAMBLING KING...
...WHY DOESN'T HE FIND A NEW HOBBY?
SSS... SSS...
WHAT'S HE WANT WITH THE DOJO ANYWAY ?!
MUTTER MUTTER
FLIP
NOTHING YOU CAN DO NOW, ANYWAY.
WHY DON'T YOU STAY OVER TONIGHT?
I'LL TAKE GOOD CARE OF YA!
BAP
ST -ST -STAY OVER... T - TONIGHT... ?!
SIZZZZLE
OKONOMIYAKI
UCCHAN'S

PART 10
NEVER BET YOUR LIFE

OOOO
BOW WOW WOW
...RANMA ACTUALLY BET THE WHOLE DOJO?
YES.
FATHER SEEMS VERY UPSET.
......
WHAT ARE RANMA AND UKYO THINKING?!
YOU CAN'T GO HOME, RIGHT?
SO JUST STAY HERE TONIGHT.
THANKS, UCCHAN.
OKAY, SO THEY'RE CHILDHOOD FRIENDS... BUT THEY'RE STILL A BOY AND GIRL, AFTER ALL...
ALTHOUGH...WITH THOSE TWO, SOMETIMES IT'S HARD TO TELL...

I WONDER WHAT RANMA IS GOING TO *DO?*
MAYBE HE'LL JUST SWITCH OVER TO UKYO NOW.
WHY WOULD HE DO THAT?
WELL, SHE'S HIS FIANCÉE TOO, RIGHT?
TRUE. AND SHE'S A COOK...
AND HE *DOES* LOVE FOOD...
AHEM IN ANY CASE, AKANE, HERE'S A CHANGE OF CLOTHES FOR HIM.
HUH?
WELL, I THOUGHT THAT SINCE RANMA MAY BE STAYING WITH UKYO FOR A WHILE...
.....
RANMA, YOU JERK!
EVERYTHING WAS FINE 'TIL YOU CAME ALONG...
MUTTER MUTTER
TOLL FREE!
CREE CREE CREE

HE CAN DO ANYTHING HE WANTS, FOR ALL I CARE.
MAYBE HE'LL JUST SWITCH OVER TO UKYO NOW.
WHAT'S THERE TO THINK ABOUT, RAN-CHAN?
HEY, RAN--
HOW CARE-LESS.
IT'S OPEN...
KRAA
ORANGES
HYUUUU...
OKONOMIYAKI UCCHAN'S
CLOSED
COME AGAIN!
I'M TIRED OF WAITING...
PERK
ERRRGH...
WHICH IS IT GOING TO BE?
BE A MAN AND MAKE YOUR CHOICE!
BUT I DON'T KNOW WHICH TO GIVE UP.

HE'S...
HE'S CHOOSING WHICH OF US TO MARRY...! HE'S ABOUT TO...
--OKAY! THE ONE I WANT IS RIGHT HERE!
AT LAST! ♪
WHAT?!
RAN-MAA!!
KWAAA
WHAT'S THE TROUBLE, AKANE?
OH... NOTHING...

"GAMBLING TRAINING"?
YEAH.
YOU JUST WATCH GAMBLING KING. THE DOJO I LOST GAMBLING I'LL WIN BACK BY GAMBLING!
GNNNNNNG
IF THAT'S WHAT IT'S FOR, I WANT TO HELP.
HA.
JUST DON'T BLAME ME IF YOU GO BANKRUPT.
SSHHFF
IF HE WANTS TO WIN BACK THE DOJO... THEN HE MIGHT WANT ...
YAY! I WIN!
ONE MORE TIME!
YAY! I WIN!
ONE MORE TIME!
ONE MORE TIME!

WHY ARE YOU GUYS SO *GOOD?*
sparkle
YOU'RE KIDDING, RIGHT... ?
THE QUESTION IS WHY ARE *YOU* SO *BAD?*
TARA TARA
B-DUM B-DUM
KING OPEN
CASINO KING OPEN
CASINO KING ?
IS IT A NEW ARCADE?
LET'S GO CHECK IT OUT!
TARA
B-DUM B-DUM

CASINO
King
FORMER TENDO DOJO...
HERE IT IS!
BLAH BLAH
OKAY, PLACE YOUR BETS!
RED!
BLACK!
YOU LOSE!
K-CHING K-CHING
OH, NO!
GARRRRRR
C'MON! C'MON!
PART-TIMING.
NABIKI, WHAT ARE YOU DOING?!

IT'S YOUR FUNERAL.
GAMBLING KING! I CHALLENGE YOU TO A MATCH FOR THE OWNERSHIP OF THE TENDO DOJO!
CAR ADVENTURE
EXPLODE!
SO?
WHAT WILL YOU GIVE ME IF YOU LOSE?
DADDY...!
YOU LOSE.
JOKER
NO LESS...THAN THE TENDO FAMILY'S LIVING ROOM!
VWAA
Entitles the bearer to ownership of the Tendo Living Room. Signed, Soun Tendo
GAMBLING KING! THIS TIME I CHALLENGE YOU!

HEH HEH HEH!
NOW YOU'LL SEE WHAT *TRAINING* CAN DO!
SSHHFF...
I WISH I FELT MORE SECURE...
I'M COUNTING ON YOU, SON!
Sobb
BAH!
LEAVE IT TO ME.
I BET NO LESS... THAN THE TENDO FAMILY'S FRONT PORCH!
SLAM
Entitles
Beare
Tend
Front Porch.
Ranma Saotome
YOU LOSE.
YOU FOOL!
DA-KRROOOM

I'LL HAVE TO DO THIS MYSELF!
HOW COULD I LEAVE IT TO THAT TWERP?!
HOLD IT RIGHT THERE!
NABIKI'S ROOM!
YOU LOSE.
AKANE'S ROOM!
TENDO HALLWAY!
STAIRS!
BATH-ROOM!
Tendo
TENDO KITCHEN!
YOU LOSE.
FEH...
LET'S PLAY!!
SHAKE SHAKE
FATHER, IT'S TIME TO STOP.
SHALL WE GO AGAIN?
WOW, NABIKI! YOU DID IT!
ERK!
YOU LOSE!
I'LL TAKE YOU FOR ALL YOU HAVE.
NO MATTER WHO CHALLENGES ME, IT WILL BE THE SAME.
JOKER

SHE... SHE BEAT ME...
SHE DID WHAT NO ONE ELSE HAS BEEN ABLE TO...
PAST VICTIMS
BUT THEN...SHE *IS* IN HIGH SCHOOL!
GRRRRR
MAYBE HE CAN'T BEAT ANYONE WHO KNOWS MORE THAN AN ELEMENTARY-SCHOOL STUDENT...
THAT WOULD FIT THE FACTS...
--AND WHAT DOES THAT SAY ABOUT *ME?!*
SHOULD I SPELL IT?
THROW IN RANMA, TOO...
THE LIVING ROOM IS *MINE!*
FWAP
ARRGH!
Soun Tendo
Tendo
THE ONLY THING LEFT IS THE DOJO!
THIS IS THE LAST STAND...FOR MY *PRIDE!*

LET'S PLAY !!
ONLY ONE THING LEFT TO DO!
WELCOME TO UCCHAN'S!
KRAAAAA
Ucchan's
YEP. SHE'S NOW HERE.
MMM... CUTE WAITRESS !
TEE HEE

YOU'VE GOT A LOT MORE WORK TO DO TO PAY OFF YOUR LOSSES FROM YOUR "TRAINING."
SHAKKA SHAKKA
IOU one hour work per 1000 yen bet. R Saotome
GAMBLING... IS MY RUIN...
Sob
PUBLIC BATHS
BLIC BATHS
MEANTIME, LET'S KEEP UP THE TRAINING.
HMM...
COIN LAUNDRY
N MONEY at HOME
RAN-CHAN... IS IT POSSIBLE...

...YOU WANT TO GO BACK TO AKANE'S PLACE?
WHA-- ?
OF COURSE NOT !
ANY-HOW...
I CAN'T GO BACK UNTIL I BEAT THAT "KING"!
REALLY ?
I HAVE TO BEAT HIM!
I'M GOING TO STAY HERE UNTIL I *DO!*
GRRR
OH, RANMA !
THAT MEANS YOU'LL LIVE WITH ME *FOREVER!*
MONTHLY PARKING
SEE ATTENDANT
SKWEE
MEANING EXACTLY... *WHAT?*
SUDDENLY I HAVE SO MUCH TIME...
SO MUCH TIME TO WIN RAN-CHAN'S HEART!

YOU ONLY HAD TO WIN *ONE* MORE... HOW *COULD* YOU?!
LIKE I SAID... HE CHEATED!
WHATEVER THE REASON...WE HAVE TO MOVE OUT OF OUR HOUSE.
boohoohoo
WHAT LOSERS.
Crowded, ain't it.
HEY, *YOU* STARTED THIS MESS, RANMA!
YEAH...AND *I'M* GONNA *END* IT!
COME AND GET ME, PEASANTS!

PART 11
PUT ON A POKER FACE

RANMA SAOTOME!
AKANE TENDO!
UKYO KUONJI...
...ARE THEY ALL ABSENT?
HUH? THEY'RE GONE.
THEY WERE JUST THERE SLEEPING.
I'M DONE!
ME TOO!
AARGH!
RAN-CHAN... THERE'S NEVER BEEN A PLAYER AS BAD AS YOU.
BUT YOUR FACE-OFF WITH THE KING IS AFTER SCHOOL!

I WISH MY WHOLE FAMILY DIDN'T HAVE TO COME...
PRRRRRR
YOU'RE WELCOME TO GO...AND LEAVE RAN-CHAN.
WE CAN'T ALL STAY AT UKYO'S HOUSE FOREVER YOU KNOW...
SHP SHP
HOW CAN YOU BE SO POSITIVE?
OH, WILL YOU STOP WORRYING?! I'M GONNA WIN BACK YOUR HOUSE *AND* DOJO!
NABIKI...?
WANT ME TO TELL YOU HOW TO BEAT HIM...?

I'M THE ONLY ONE WHO'S EVER BEATEN HIM, RIGHT?
HE CHEATED, AND BEAT ME AT THE END...
BUT WHILE I WAS PLAYING...
I NOTICED A HABIT THAT THIS "KING" HAS...
A HABIT... !?
YES! FOR EXAMPLE...
SHA
IF YOU PUSH UP THE OLD MAID...
...JUST A LITTLE...
...LIKE THIS, SO IT'S EASY TO GRAB...
JOKER
JOKER

HE ALWAYS PICKS THAT CARD!
IS THAT TRUE !?
JOKER
YOU'VE GOT TO BE KIDDING ME! NOBODY OVER *SIX* WOULD FALL FOR A TRICK LIKE THAT!
PIK
WHAT WAS THAT... LITTLE RANMA?
ping!
AND THAT'S NOT ALL. HE'S GOT ANOTHER FATAL WEAKNESS!
WH- WH- WHAT'S THAT !?

WHEN THE KING IS HOLDING THE OLD MAID...
GLINT
...AND YOU PLACE YOUR HAND ON IT...
...HE STARTS TO LOOK REALLY HAPPY.
SO YOU SWITCH TO A DIFFERENT CARD...
...AND THEN HE LOOKS LIKE THE END OF THE WORLD IS COMING.
OF COURSE... HE'S NOT THE ONLY ONE.
HYUUUUU...
NO WONDER HE CAN'T WIN.

PWAAAA
K-TAK K-TAK
CASINO King
SHA
DADDY'S GOTTEN BETTER, RIGHT?
WELL... HE *SAYS* HE HAS...
I CHALLENGE YOU!

WE'VE COME TO RECLAIM OUR HOME...
...AND OUR DOJO!
SO, YOU'VE COME FOR ANOTHER BEATING, EH, PEASANTS?
いろは
WELL...
AKANE, WHERE'S RANMA?
EASIER SAID THAN DONE...
JUST DRAG THE MATCH OUT UNTIL THEN.
I'LL BE THERE...AS SOON AS I GET RID OF THIS WEAKNESS!

LET'S PLAY !!
YOU ARE ALL DOOMED.
HURRY RANMA...
EVEN IF YOU WON'T DO ANY GOOD...
VMMM
heh
ping

YOU'RE JUST NOT MADE FOR GAMBLING.
I WON'T GIVE UP!
THAT'LL KEEP HAPPENING...AS LONG AS YOU KEEP REACTING.
MOOSH
5K
I CAN'T STOP THIS TRAINING UNTIL I HAVE NO FACIAL EXPRESSIONS AT ALL!
I'M TAKING MY ROOM BACK!
FWA
I WIN!
Entitles Bearer to Nabiki's Bedroom. Signed, Soun Tendo
CASINO King

AND SO DO I! I'LL TAKE THE KITCHEN.
Entitles Bearer to
AND ME!
I'LL TAKE BACK MY ROOM.
Entitles Bearer to Akane's room
WELL DONE!
THAT'S MY GIRLS!
YOU LOSE.
DAAA-DDY!
ONE MORE GAME!
SHP SHP
THE LIVING ROOM IS MINE!
THE BATH-ROOM IS MINE!
THE PORCH IS MINE!
ONE MORE GAME!
I WIN!
I'VE GOT THE STAIRS!
I HAVE THE HALL-WAYS...
...AND I HAVE THE YARD!
CAR ADVENTURE
WELL...THAT'S THE WHOLE HOUSE. SHALL WE GO?
YES.
I SHOULD START MAKING DINNER SOON.
FWAP

THE ONLY THING LEFT IS THE *DOJO!*
I BET THE *LIVING ROOM!*
SKREEK
BAM
Entitles Bearer to
DADDY, IF YOU DO THAT *ONE MORE TIME--*
DM DM DM DM
EEYAGGA...!
ENOUGH IS ENOUGH, FATHER.
DAD!
LET *ME* DO IT!
AKANE...
ZIP
Entitles bearer to Akane's room. Signed, Soun Tendo
WELL, RANMA... YOU NEVER MADE IT...
SO NOW...

...IT'S ALL UP TO *ME!*
LET'S PLAY!
STOP !
I'M TAKING OVER.
SHMM
THE VICTORY... WILL BE *MINE.*
WE ALMOST MADE IT ...
OH, NOOO.

RANMA... LEVEL WITH US...
HAVE YOU ACTUALLY GOTTEN ANY BETTER?
NOT ONE LITTLE, TINY BIT.
CRA DRIVER
NONE ?!
NO MATTER WHAT, THE EXPRESSIONS KEPT COMING.
YES.
BUT THANKS TO THE TRAINING...
5K
...AT LEAST NOW YOU CAN'T *SEE* MY EXPRESSIONS!
ta-DAA
GASP! HE'S RIGHT!
TALK ABOUT PUTTING ON A GAME FACE...!
WHAT A SACRI-FICE...

ALL RIGHT, RANMA SAOTOME!
PAM
BECAUSE OF YOUR DETERMINATION...I AGREE TO A ONE-ON-ONE MATCH WITH YOU.
HUH...?
YOU'VE GOT IT.
I DON'T TRUST THIS GUY!
HE WOULDN'T BE ACTING SO NOBLE...
erk!
...IF HE DIDN'T HAVE A *PLAN* FOR BEATING RANMA!
AND WHAT WILL YOU WAGER?
THE DEED TO UCCHAN'S OKONOMIYAKI!
HERE!
FWAP
WHA...?

UKYO, ARE YOU SURE?!
THAT'S YOUR LIVELIHOOD...
IT DOESN'T MATTER, EITHER WAY.
BECAUSE IN CASE RAN-CHAN LOSES... WE HAVE AN AGREEMENT.
AN... AGREEMENT...?
BUT... BUT WHAT CAN IT...?
YOU WILL LOSE, RANMA SAOTOME.
HEH! EVEN WITH MY EMOTIONS CONCEALED?
SMIRK
HE IS JUST *NOT* MADE FOR GAMBLING...!
HE'S SMILING!
HE SURE IS!

PART 12
THE VIRTUES OF TRAINING

NOW, IT'S ONE ON ONE...AT OLD MAID!
YADA YADA YADA
CASINO
K
I WAGER THE TENDO DOJO!
I WAGER UCCHAN'S OKONOMIYAKI!

HWOOOOOO
SHUCKS, HONEY...WE PROMISED NOT TO BRING THAT UP AGAIN, REMEMBER?
I'M SO SORRY YOU LOST YOUR BUSINESS BECAUSE OF ME...
OKONOMIYAKI
Ucchan's
SHKK SHKK
YEP.
HE PROMISED ME.
IF HE LOSES... HE'LL BECOME YOUR COOK?!
AND EVENT-UALLY...
SSHHH
YOU'RE...
...YOU'RE SO...
...SO GOOD...
...TO ME...
I ♥ U UKYO
OH, UCCHAN...
OH, RANMA...
BLUSH

OH, UCCHAN!
OH, RANMA!
IT'S MEANT TO BE!
UM... HELLO...?
WHAT A MATCH!
IT'S INCREDIBLE!
YADA YADA
VMM
HHHHSSSSSSS

C'MON... TAKE THE OLD MAID!
NYU
JOKER
HA HA! GOT YOU!
OH, NO!
GASP
TRY THIS!
NYU
JOKER
THE JOKER! AGAIN!
YAAGH!
SMIRK
THEY'RE PASSING THE JOKER BACK AND FORTH!
YES... YES!
THEY'RE BOTH--
THE TWO OF THEM ARE EQUALLY MATCHED!

EQUALLY STUPID !!
HHHHSSSSSSS
WAIT A SECOND !
THAT'S--
FOR SOME REASON... THAT'S THE ONLY SCUFFED CARD...
JOKER
2
--I'VE GOT IT!
BY SLIPPING THE JOKER BACK AND FORTH FOR HOURS...

JOKER
...YOU'RE HOPING TO WEAR ME DOWN!
I'VE SEEN THROUGH YOUR TECHNIQUE!
SHWA!
OOOO!!
!
JOKER
HEH HEH HEH...
I WON'T BE TAKING THE JOKER *THIS* TIME!
GACK!!
HEH.
JOKER

WHY, THAT -- !
WHILE RANMA WAS BUSY DRAWING A CARD...
...THE KING SLIPPED THE OLD MAID INTO HIS HAND!
HE'S CHEATING!
IS THAT WHAT HAPPENED ?!
FASTER THAN THE EYE COULD FOLLOW!
QUIT IT, AKANE!
BUT... BUT...
COME ON, KING! TAKE A CARD!
NYU
JOKER
FEH.
I COMMEND YOU, RANMA SAOTOME.
GLARE
BUT I WILL NOT GO DOWN EASILY!

KNOW THE FOLLY OF CHALLENGING THE GAMBLING KING!
KWONK
TANG
KSSHH
TAK
ZZNGZZNG ZZNG ZZNG
WHY... YOU... LITTLE...
POIK
PING
MOOSH
ALL RIGHT, THEN...
GRRR

TAKE THIS! JOKER SHOWER!
FWOOOSHHHH
!
JOKER
JOKER
PA PA
OH, YEAH ?!
JOKER
JOKER
HUH ?!
MNCH MNCH GULP
HE ATE ALL THE JOKERS!
AMAZING !
OHHH!
THE GAME'S GETTING OUT OF CONTROL!
AND THAT'S WHEN RANMA'S AT HIS BEST!

n?
HEY KING...
EH?
WH-WHAT'S THE MATTER WITH HIM...?
RANMA-HONEY LOOKS SO...SO SAD!
Hit 'im!
ALL I WANTED...
WAS TO PLAY ONE FAIR GAME WITH YOU...
...TO PROVE I COULD BEAT YOU...
GNNG

I TRAINED FOR WEEKS!
WAAAA!
B-BUT YOU... YOU HADDA...
R-RANMA...
I DIDN'T KNOW HE CARED SO MUCH ABOUT CARDS...
YOU MEAN... I WAS YOUR PERSONAL TEST...?
GAAAAASP
I'M...
SOBB
I'M SORRY, RANMA SAOTOME!
BONK
THEN...YOU UNDERSTAND...!

HERE ARE TWO CARDS.
JOKER
A
A
fwa
PAP
SH SH SH
OKAY !
GWII
IF YOU PICK THE JOKER, YOU LOSE.
FAIR AND SQUARE.
GLMP!

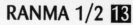

HERE GOES !
SHH
SMIRK
CAN IT BE...?
THE KING'S SMILING !
HE MUST HAVE SWITCHED THE CARDS...SO THAT THEY'RE *BOTH* JOKERS!
HE'S CHEATING !
RANMA, DON'T PICK A CARD!
SHWA

HWOOOOOOO
RANMA...
TROMP TROMP
SHH-H
I WIN.
heh
FWIP
OH... RANMA! SON!
HUH?
SOBB SOBB
CLAP CLAP CLAP CLAP
PING

END OF RANMA 1/2 VOLUME 13.

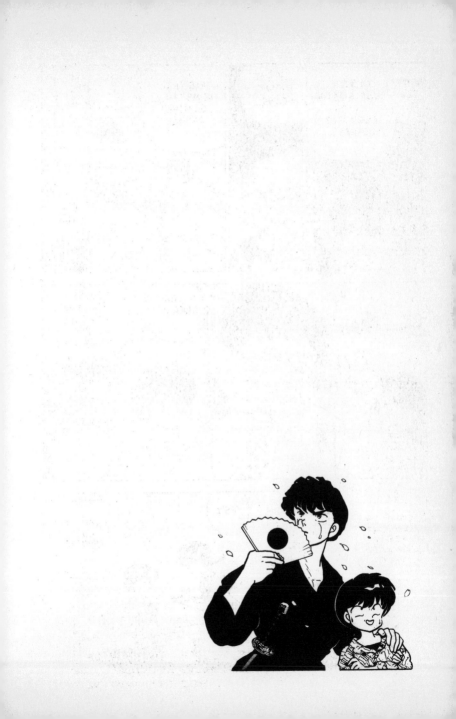

About Rumiko Takahashi

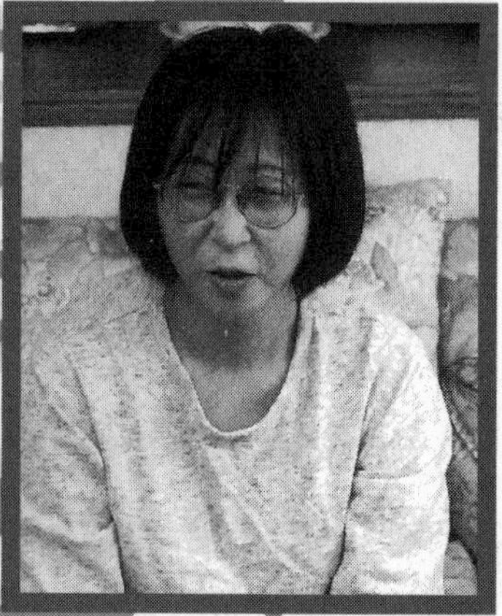

Born in 1957 in Niigata, Japan, Rumiko Takahashi attended women's college in Tokyo, where she began studying comics with Kazuo Koike, author of CRYING FREEMAN. She later became an assistant to horror-manga artist Kazuo Umezu (OROCHI). In 1978, she won a prize in Shogakukan's annual "New Comic Artist Contest," and in that same year her boy-meets-alien comedy series URUSEI YATSURA began appearing in the weekly manga magazine SHÔNEN SUNDAY. This phenomenally successful series ran for nine years and sold over 22 million copies. Takahashi's later RANMA 1/2 series enjoyed even greater popularity.

Takahashi is considered by many to be one of the world's most popular manga artists. With the publication of Volume 34 of her RANMA 1/2 series in Japan, Takahashi's total sales passed one hundred million copies of her compiled works.

Takahashi's serial titles include URUSEI YATSURA, RANMA 1/2, ONE-POUND GOSPEL, MAISON IKKOKU and INUYASHA. Additionally, Takahashi has drawn many short stories which have been published in America under the title "Rumic Theater," and several installments of a saga known as her "Mermaid" series. Most of Takahashi's major stories have also been animated, and are widely available in translation worldwide. INUYASHA is her most recent serial story, first published in SHÔNEN SUNDAY in 1996.

EDITOR'S RECOMMENDATIONS

InuYasha Ani-Manga

The story you've come to love using actual frames of film in full color from the TV and video series *Inuyasha*!

Mermaid Saga

This is the series Rumiko Takahashi created as her "hobby." Unpressured by editors and deadlines, she lets her creativity flow in this romantic-horror epic. Eating the flesh of a mermaid grants eternal life. But living forever can be a blessing or a curse. Immortal lovers Yuta and Mana are relatively lucky...others who partake of the mermaid's flesh are transformed into savage lost souls!

Inuyasha

When high-school student Kagome is transported back in time to Japan's feudal era, she accidentally releases the feral half-demon dog-boy Inu-Yasha from his imprisonment for stealing the "Jewel of Four Souls." But after a battle with fearsome demons, the jewel has been shattered and its countless shards scattered all over Japan. Now, bound together by a spell, Inu-Yasha and Kagome must join forces to reclaim the jewel and its terrifying powers from demons and mortals alike that would use it as a tool of unspeakable evil!

"Takahashi's best gift might be that of characterization...it's no wonder these stories are so universally loved."

—Courtesy of Amazon.com. All rights reserved.

InuYasha™

Rated #1 on Cartoon Network's Adult Swim!

maison ikkoku™

The beloved romantic comedy of errors—a fan favorite!

Ranma ½™

The zany, wacky study of martial arts at its best!

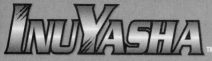

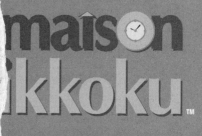